ROCK

GOT

By Aja La'Starr

Printed By
CreateSpace

ISBN-13: 978-1722094218

I would like to dedicate this book to
my college classmate
Anthony Sharp for reminding me
why the poem, "Rock What You Got" is
so important to humanity.

I would also like to dedicate this book to
my legends in the making:
Michelle, Jaylon, Lil' Marlon, Egypt, Kavi,
Levi, Kyree, Malachi, Josiah, Aiden, Shane,
Gabriel, Amelia, Amarion, Courtney, Kei'Lyn,
Kriston, Stajah, Nafe & Jamarion.

Perfectly crafted

Everyone
is
UNIQUE

From the **TOP** of your **HEAD**

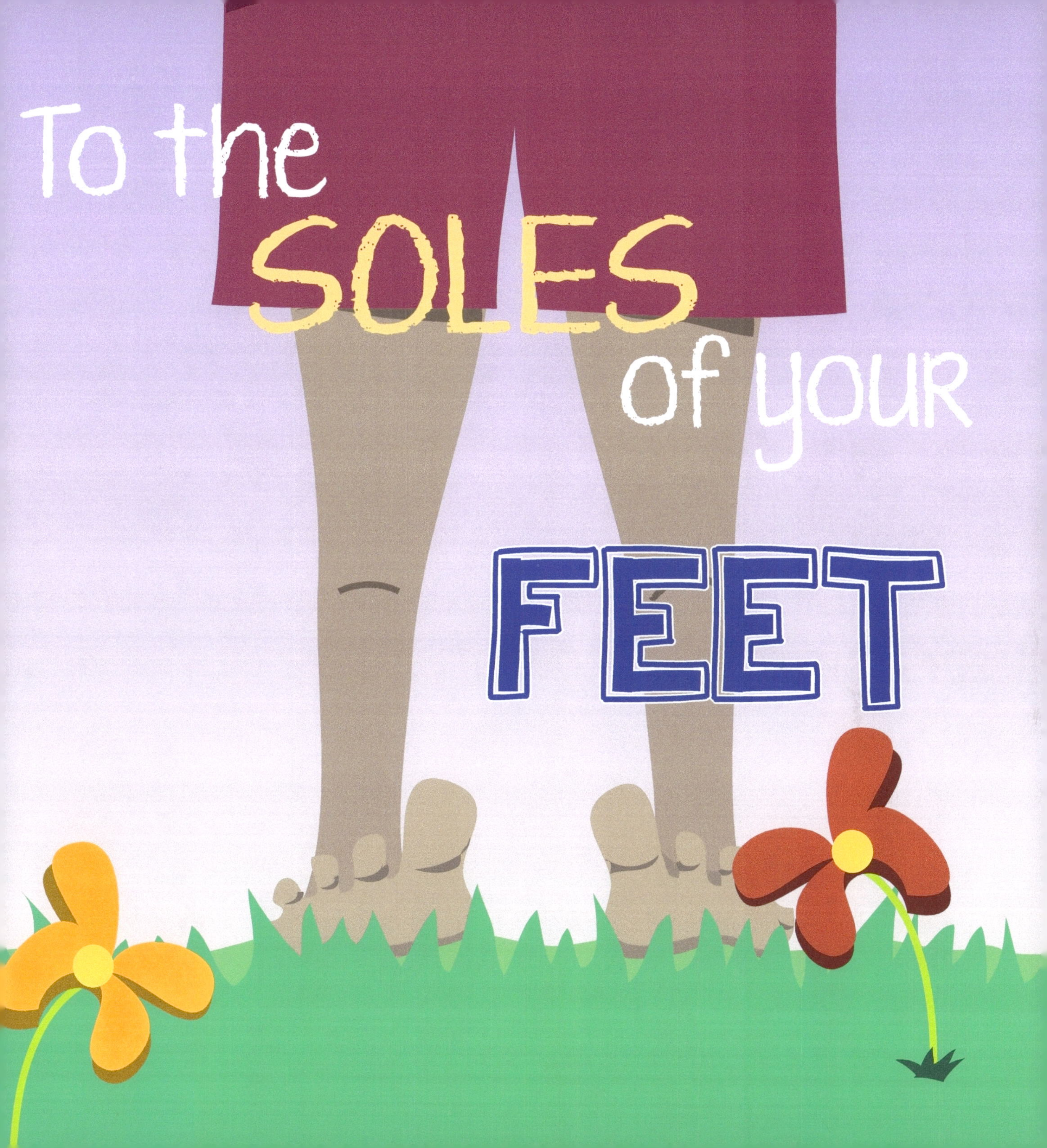

To the
SOLES
of your
FEET

From the
DIMPLE
in
your
CHEEK

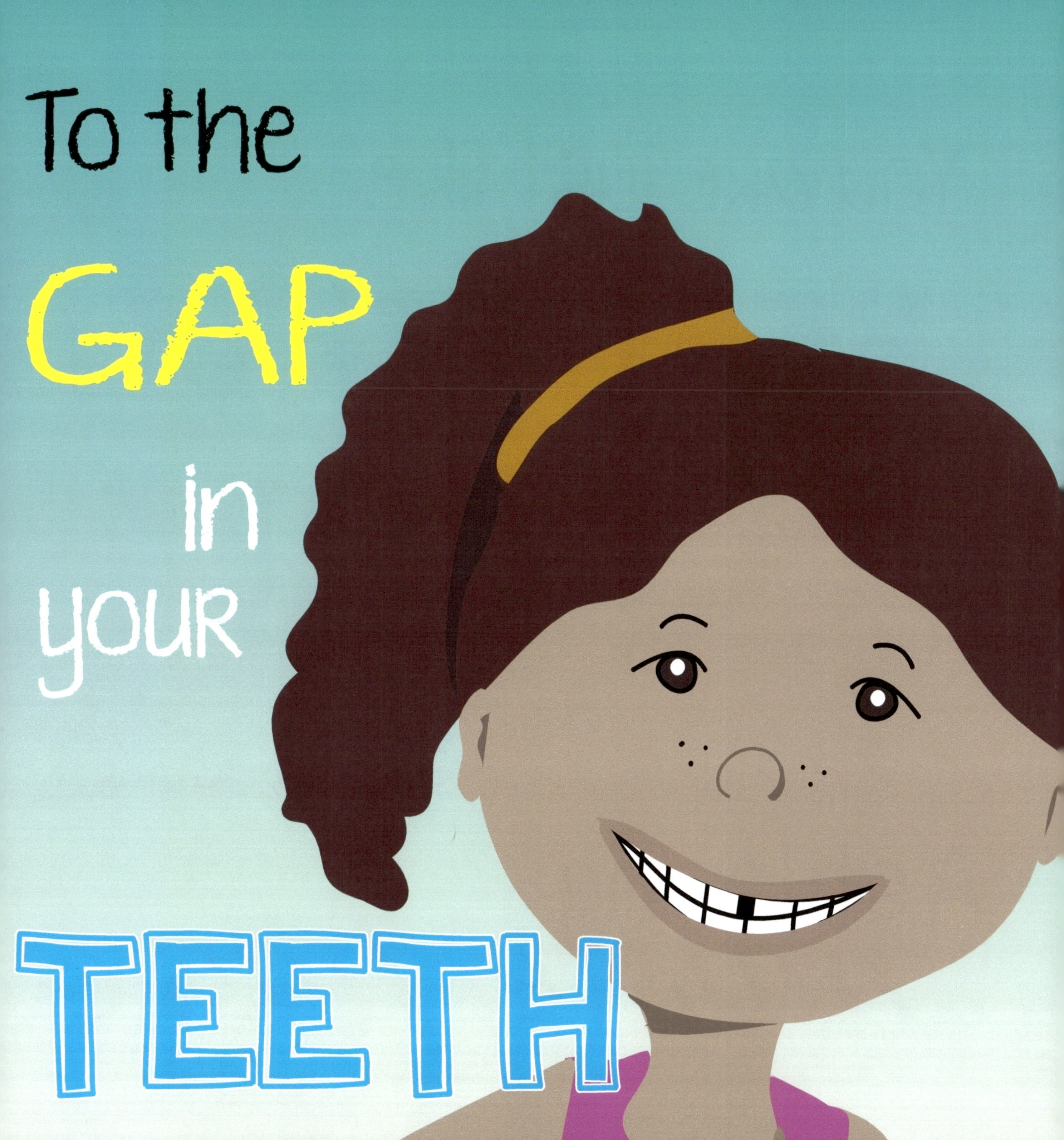

To the
GAP
in
your
TEETH

You are just like

BEAUTIFUL

ART

A stunning

masterpiece

Maybe
you
are
in
DOUBT

But you should

NEVER be

When PRECIOUS
time was
taken
out

to CREATE
who you
would
BE

From your
EYES
to your
SIZE

From
your
LIPS
to your
HIPS

From your
NOSE
to
your
EARS

Right
down
to your
FINGERTIPS

YOU
YES
YOU

Are a
STAR
in your
own
right

BUT you must

SEE

YOUR IMAGE

with your own

SIGHT

When you look
in the mirror
ALWAYS

LOVE

what you see

CELEBRATE how
GREAT
you are
and how
GREAT
you will be

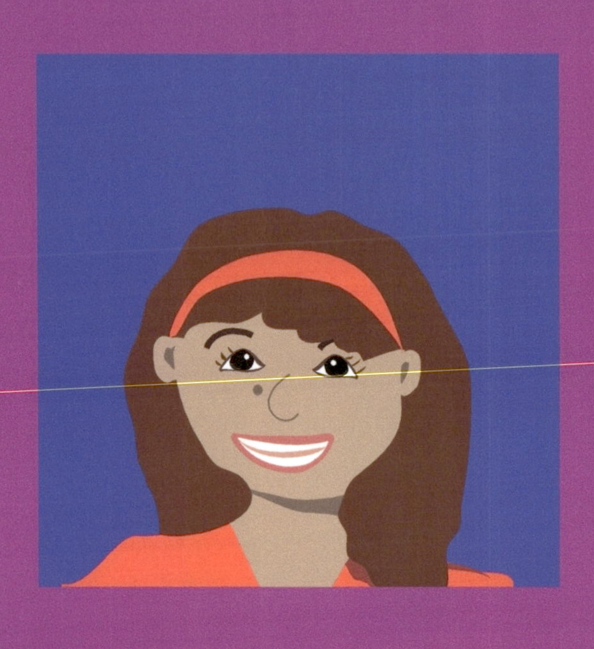

APPRECIATE
ALL of your
QUIRKS
for they are a
part of you too

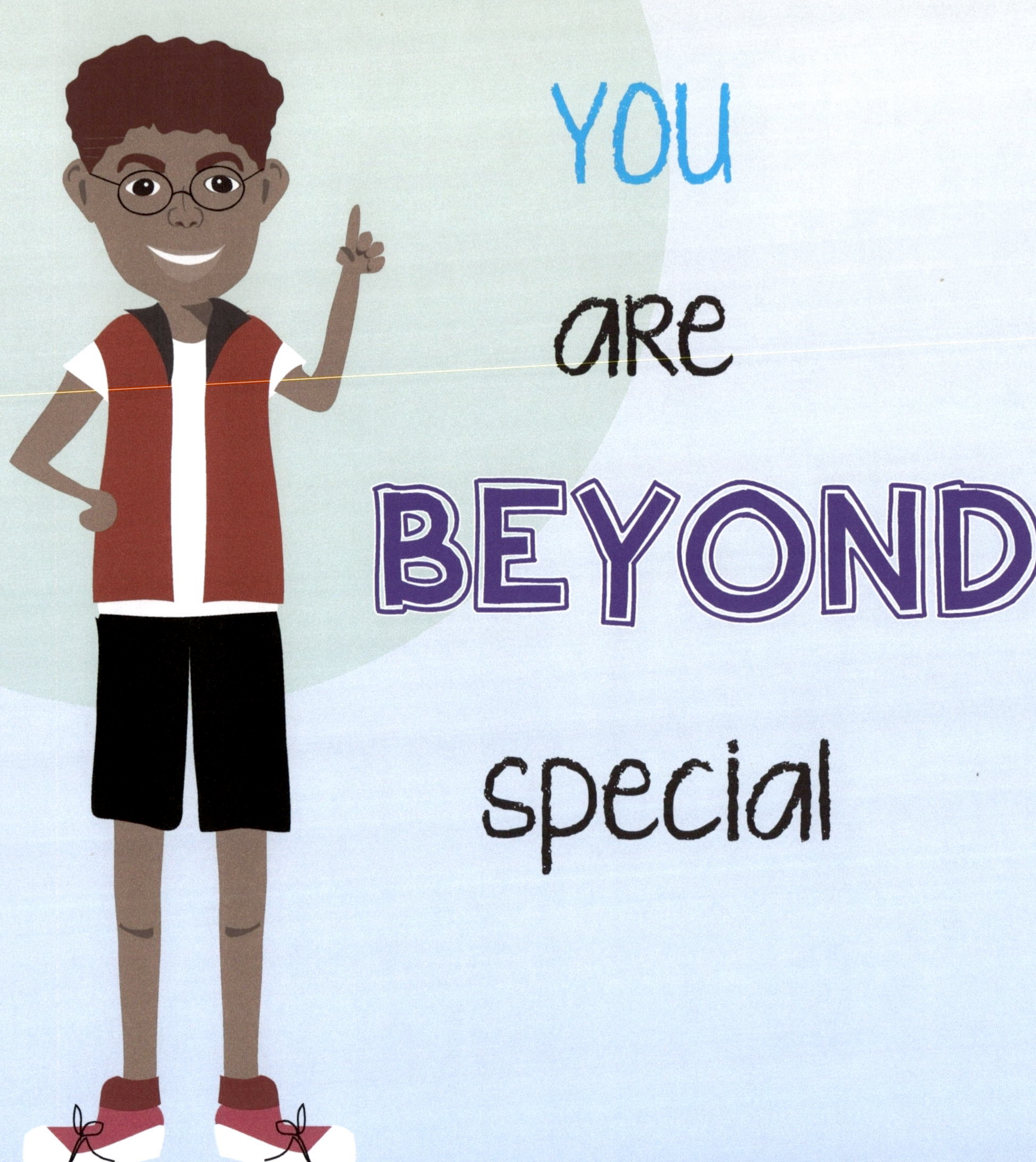

YOU
are
BEYOND
special

YOU
YES
YOU

SO

HONOR

who

you

are

because to the
WORLD
you mean
A LOT

YOU are

PERFECT

in every way

so always...

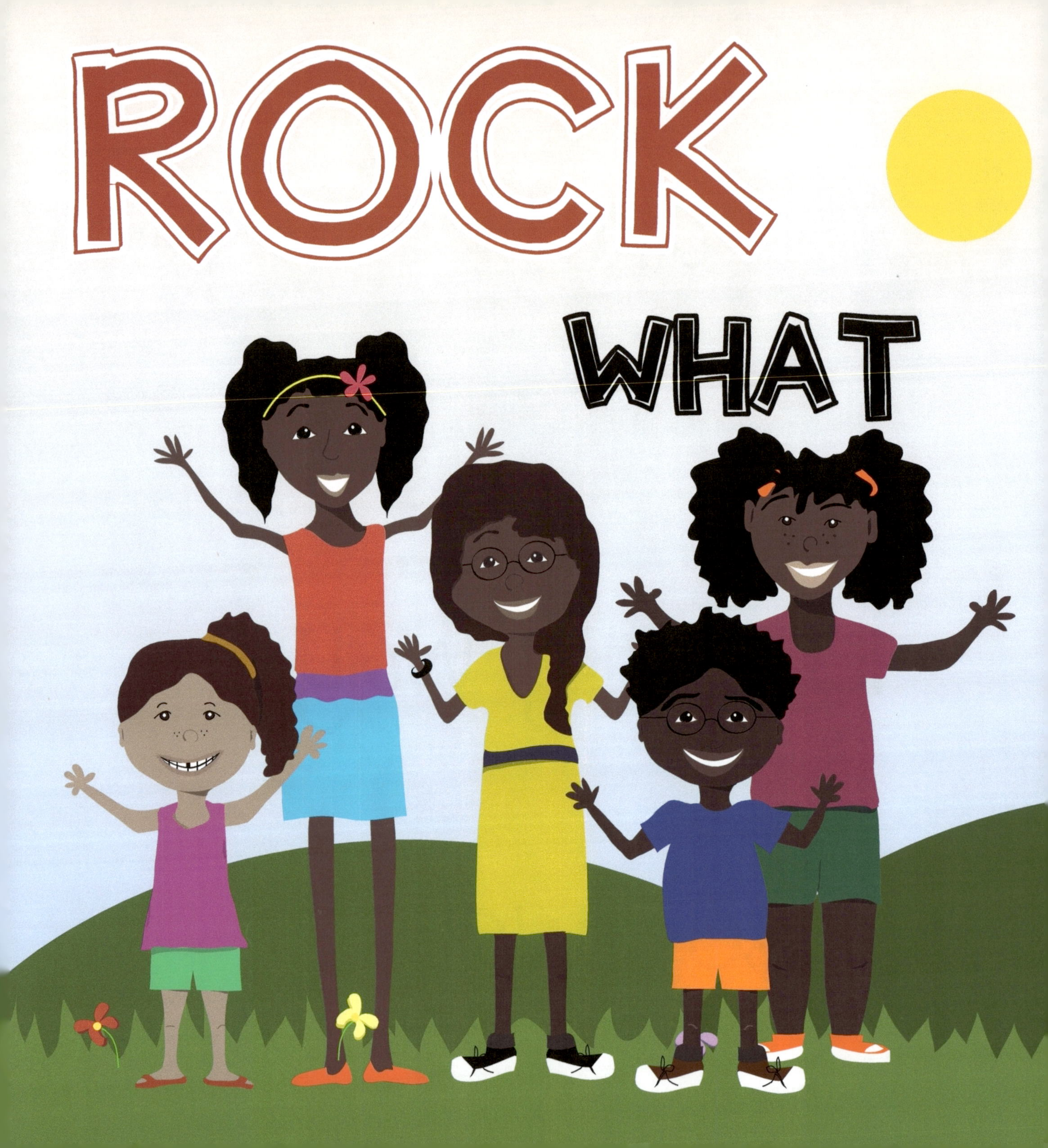

ROCK
WHAT

YOU GOT!

Discussion Questions

After you enjoy listening to or reading this book, take a moment to reflect on what "Rock What You Got" is all about.

Use the following questions to talk about the importance and value of having unique characteristics and loving your individuality!

 What does it mean to you to Rock What You Got? Name some ways that you Rock What You Got.

 Why is it important to love your unique individuality? Why is it okay to stand out from everyone else?

 Who is someone you admire or look up to who has something unique about them?

 When have you been too afraid to be who you are?

 What are some things you love most about yourself?